PIANO . VOCAL . GUITAR

T0085625

Series Artwork, Fox Trademarks and Logos
TM and © 2010 Twentieth Century Fox Film Corporation.
All Rights Reserved.

ISBN 978-1-4584-0847-1

7777 W. BLUEMOUND RD. P.O. BOX 13819 MILWAUKEE, WI 53213

Visit Hal Leonard Online at
www.halleonard.com

TEENAGE DREAM

Words and Music by LUKASZ GOTTWALD,
MAX MARTIN, BENJAMIN LEVIN,
BONNIE McKEE and KATY PERRY

Moderate Dance beat

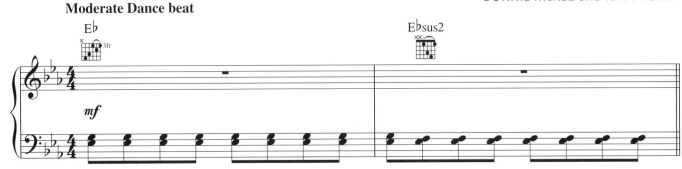

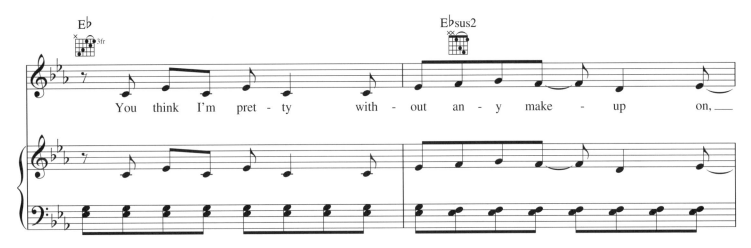

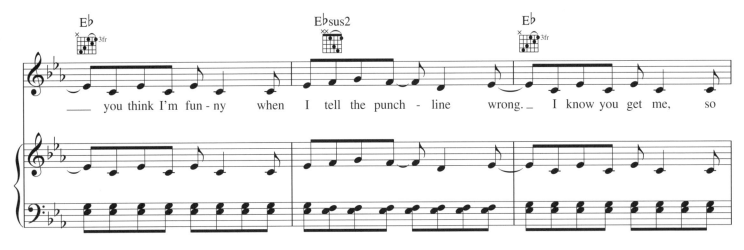

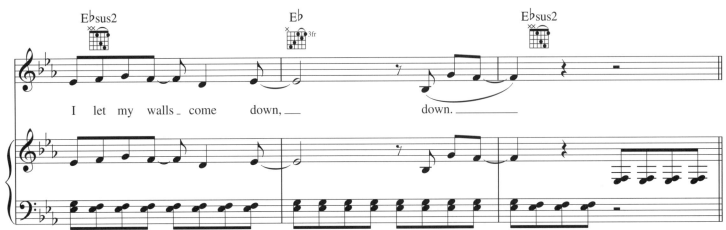

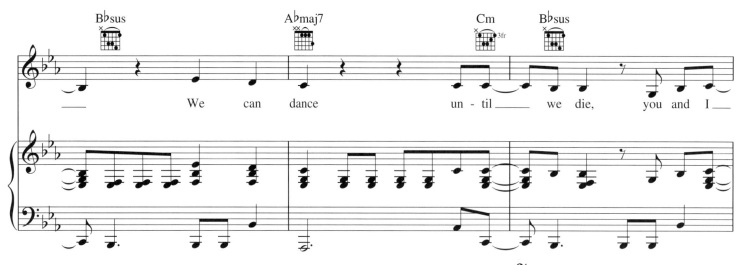

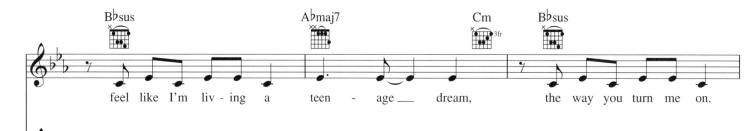

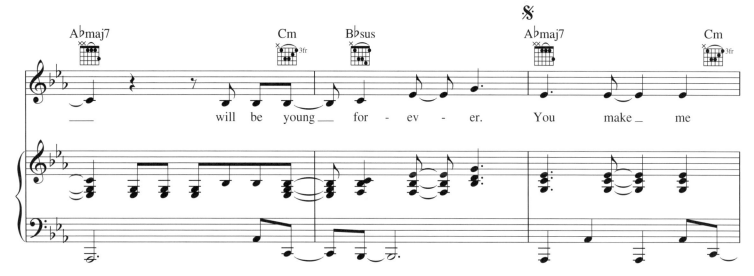

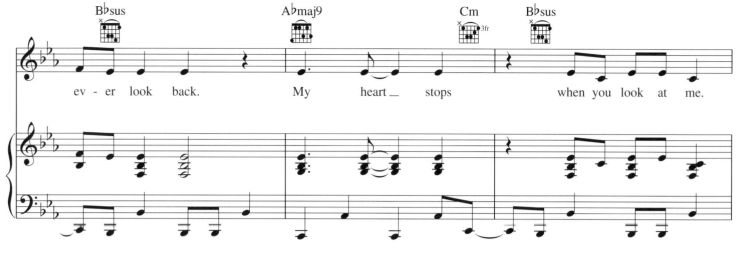

teen - age dream to - night. ___ Let you put your hands on ___ me in my

To Coda ⊕

skin - tight ___ jeans, be your teen - age dream to - night. ___

D.S. al Coda
(take 2nd ending)

You...

CODA ⊕

teen - age dream to - night. ___

HEY, SOUL SISTER

Words and Music by PAT MONAHAN,
ESPEN LIND and AMUND BJORKLAND

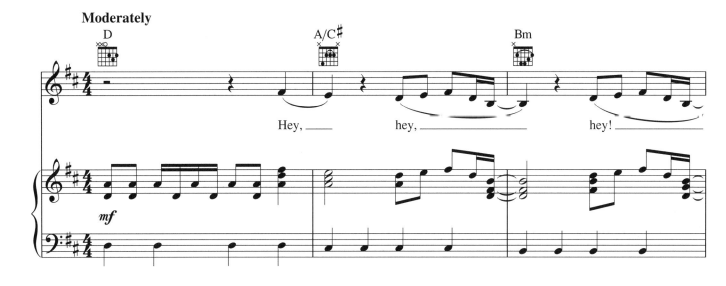

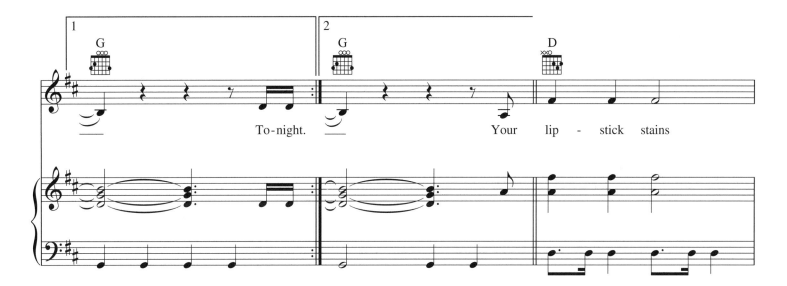

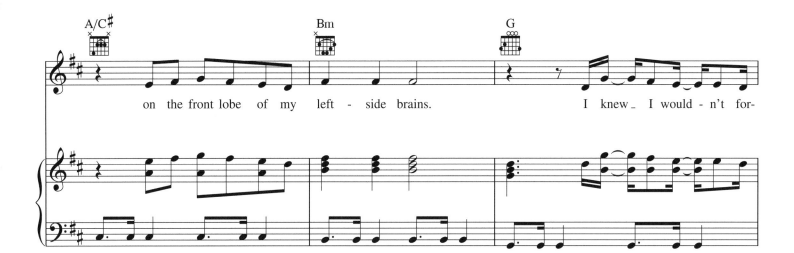

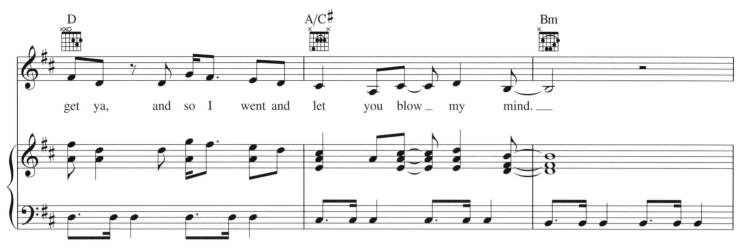

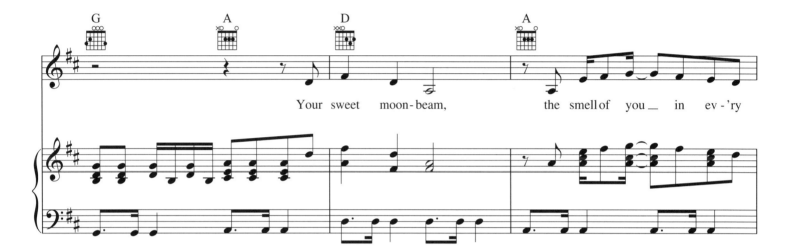

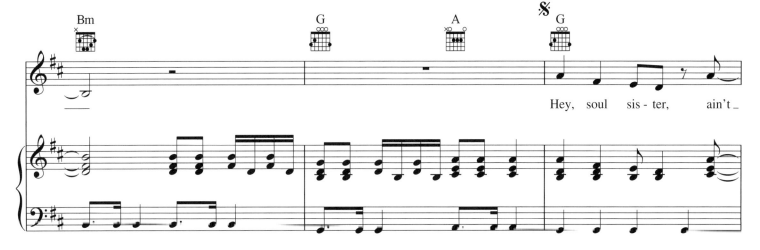

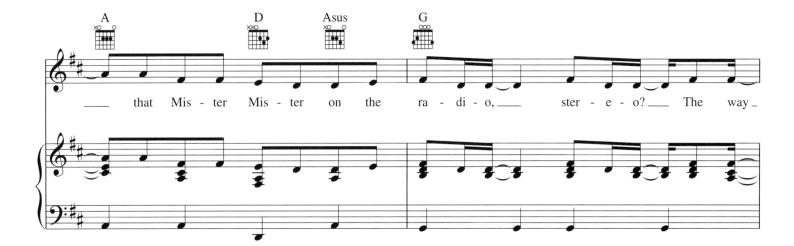

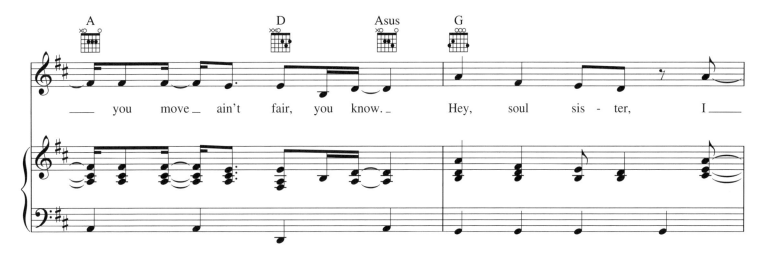

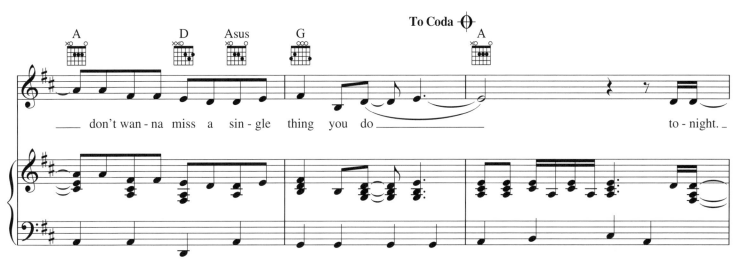

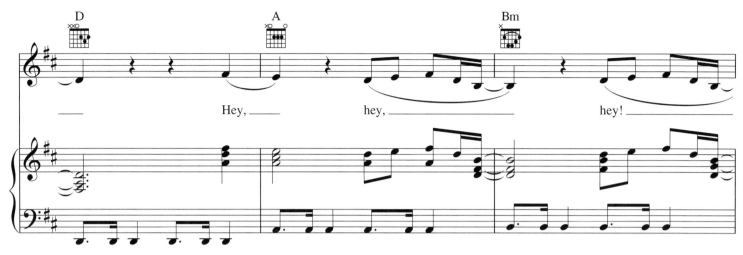

Hey, _____ hey, _____ hey! _____

_____ Just in time, _____ I'm so glad you have a

one - track mind like ___ me. _____ You gave my life di - rec -

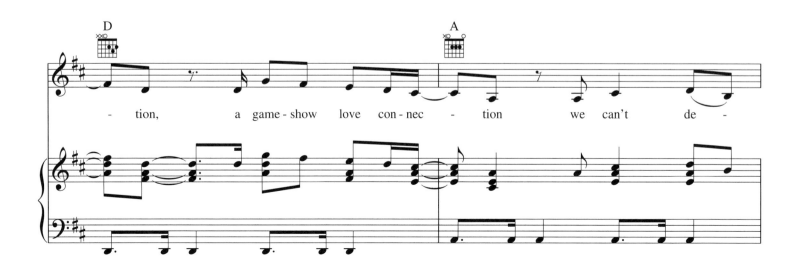

- tion, a game-show love con-nec - tion we can't de -

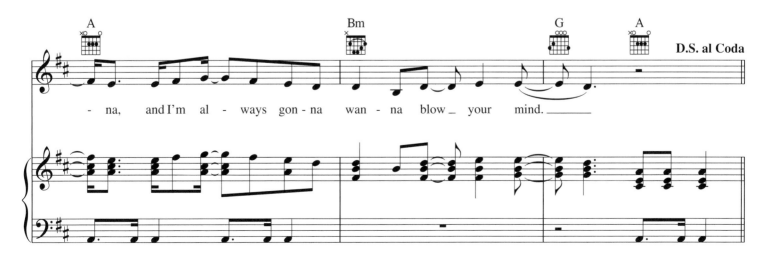

CODA

to - night. __ The way you can cut a rug, __

watch - ing you's __ the on - ly drug __ I need. __ Some gang - sta, I'm __ so thug, __ you're the

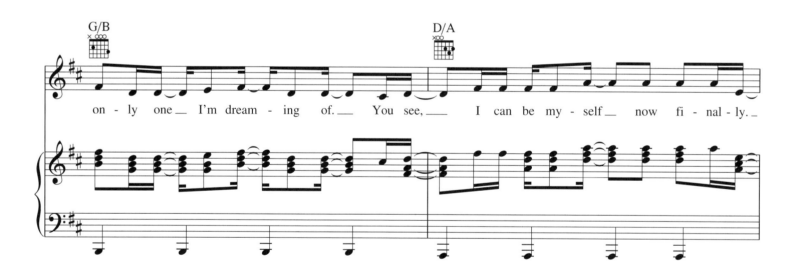

on - ly one __ I'm dream - ing of. __ You see, __ I can be my - self __ now fi - nal - ly. __

__ In fact, __ there's noth - in' I __ can't be. __ I want the world to see __ you'll

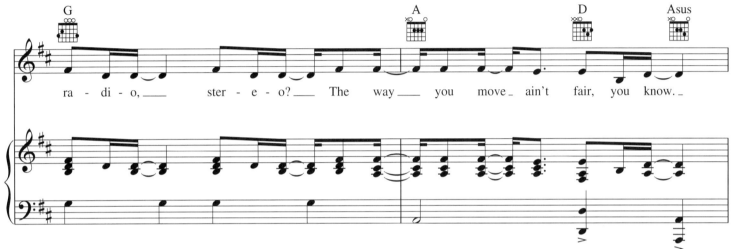

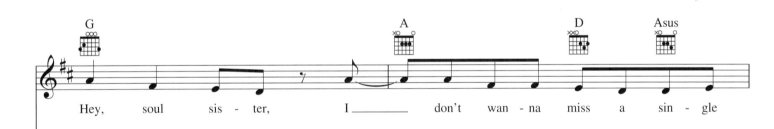

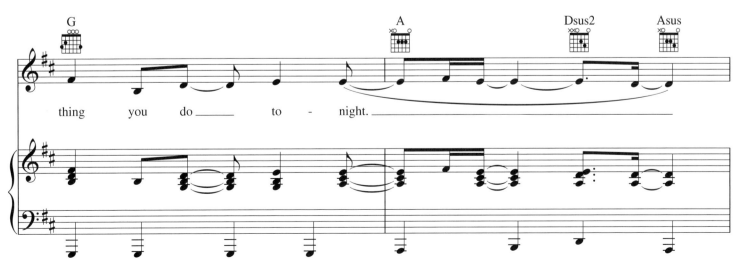

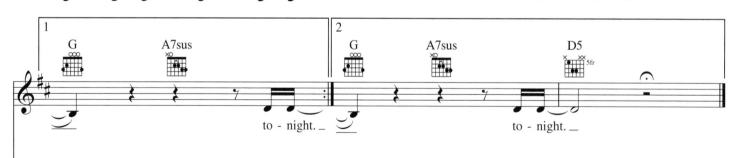

BILLS, BILLS, BILLS

Words and Music by KANDI L. BURRUSS,
KEVIN BRIGGS, BEYONCÉ KNOWLES,
KELENDRIA ROWLAND and LeTOYA LUCKETT

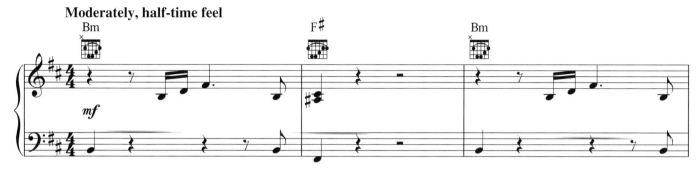

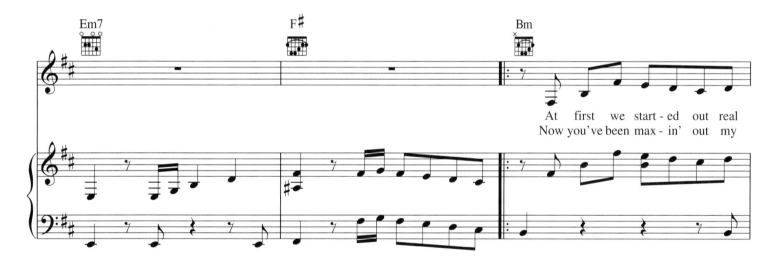

At first we start-ed out real
Now you've been max-in' out my

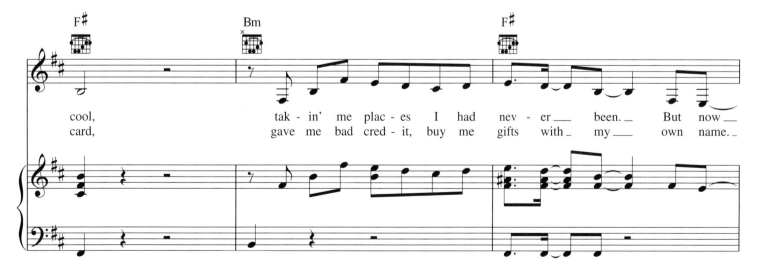

cool,   tak-in' me plac-es I had nev-er____ been.____ But now____
card,   gave me bad cred-it, buy me gifts with my____ own name.____

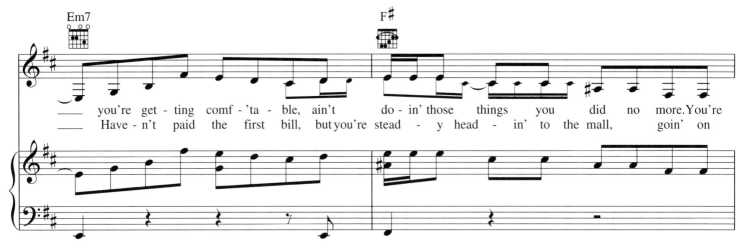

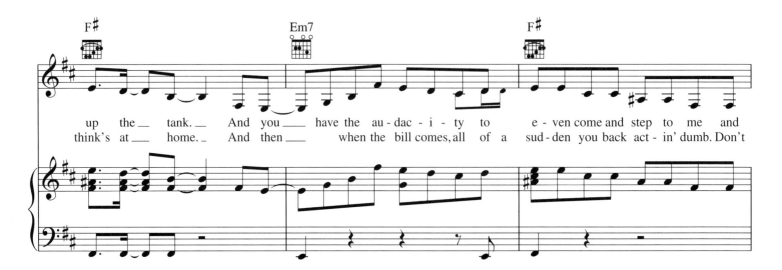

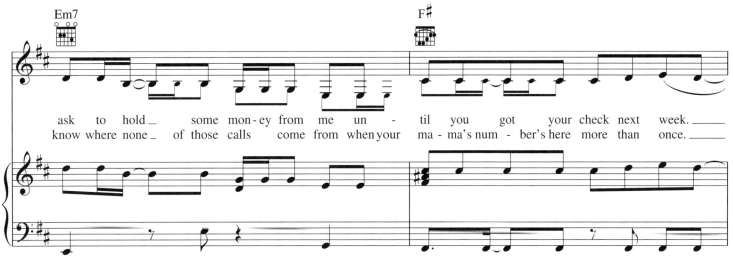

ask to hold ___ some mon-ey from me un - til you got your check next week._____

know where none _ of those calls come from when your ma - ma's num - ber's here more than once._____

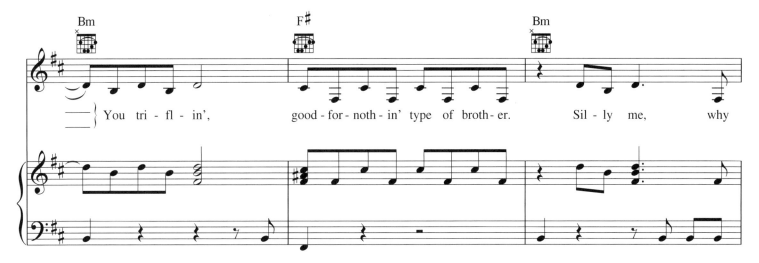

____ } You tri - fl - in', good - for - noth - in' type of broth - er. Sil - ly me, why

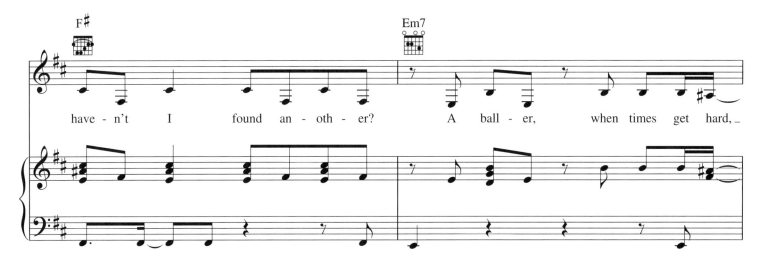

have - n't I found an - oth - er? A ball - er, when times get hard, _

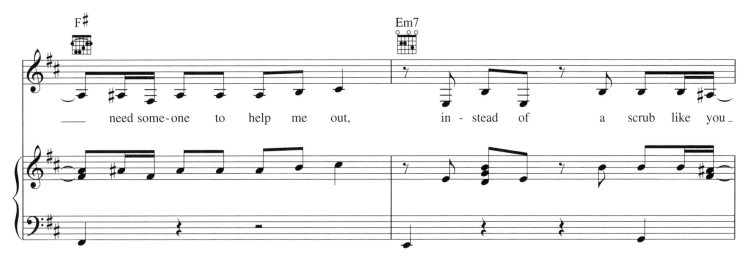

____ need some - one to help me out, in - stead of a scrub like you _

who don't know what a man's a - bout. Can you pay my bills? Can you

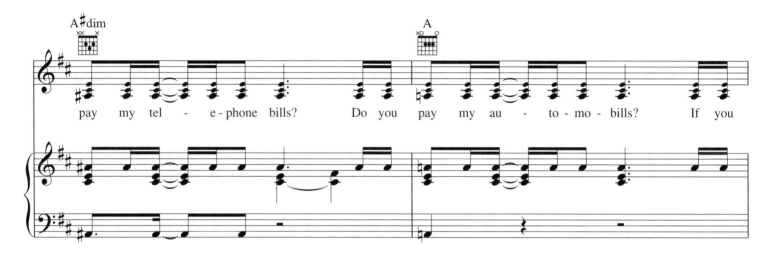

pay my tel - e - phone bills? Do you pay my au - to - mo - bills? If you

did, then may - be we could chill. I don't think you

do, so you and me are through.

You tri - fl - in' good - for - noth - in' type of broth - er. Oh, sil - ly me, why

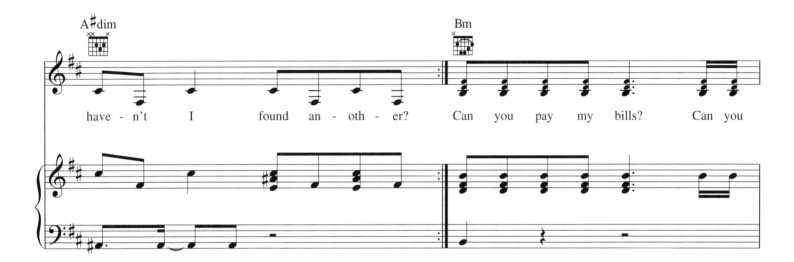

have - n't I found an - oth - er? Can you pay my bills? Can you

pay my tel - e - phone bills? Do you pay my au - to - mo - bills? If you

did, then may - be we could chill. I don't think you

do,   so   you and me are   through.

N.C.

Can   you   pay   my   bills?   Can   you   pay   my   tel - e - phone bills?   Do you

Lead vocal continue ad lib.

pay   my   au -   to - mo - bills?   If   you   did,   then   may -   be   we could chill.

I   don't   think   you   do,   so   you   and me   are   through.

SILLY LOVE SONGS

Words and Music by PAUL McCARTNEY
and LINDA McCARTNEY

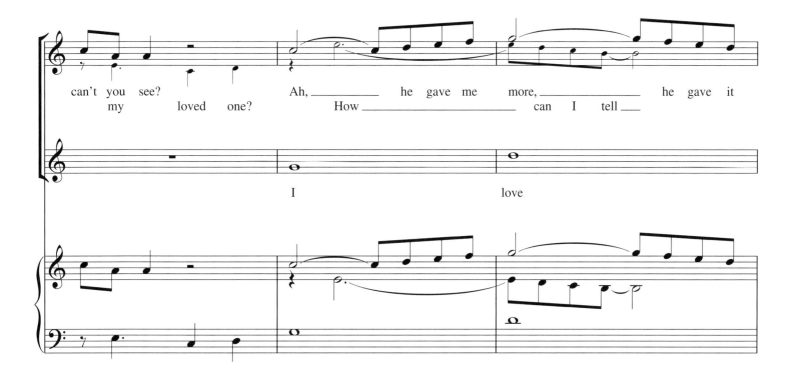

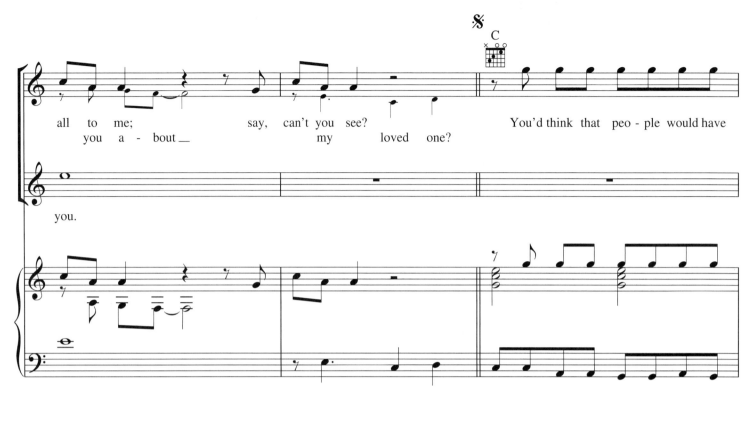

all to me; say, can't you see? You'd think that peo - ple would have
you a - bout ___ my loved one?

you.

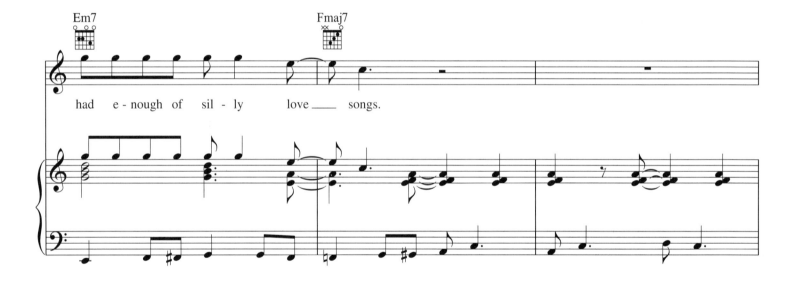

had e - nough of sil - ly love ___ songs.

But I look a - round me and I see ___ it is - n't so.

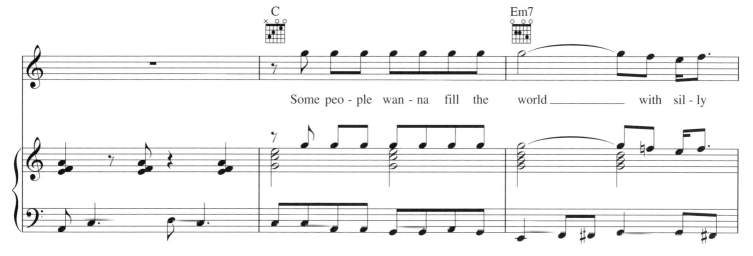

Some peo - ple wan - na fill the world _____ with sil - ly

love songs.   And what's wrong with that? _____

_____ I'd like to know, _____ 'cause

here I go _____   a - gain. _____

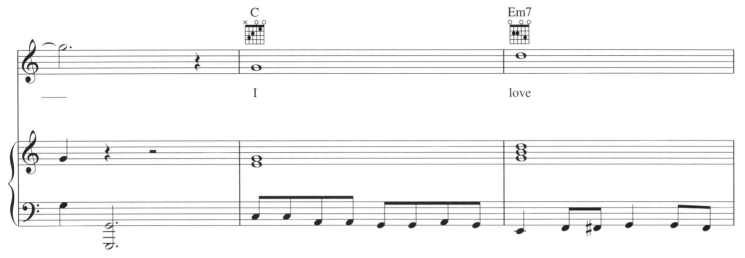

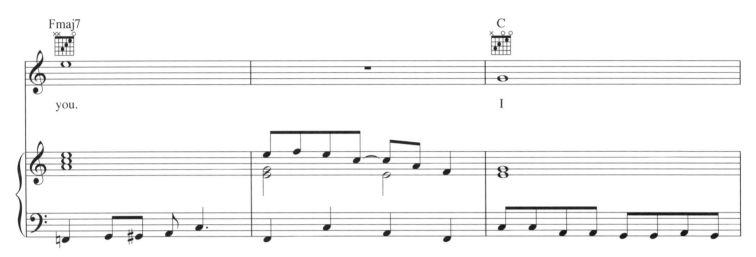

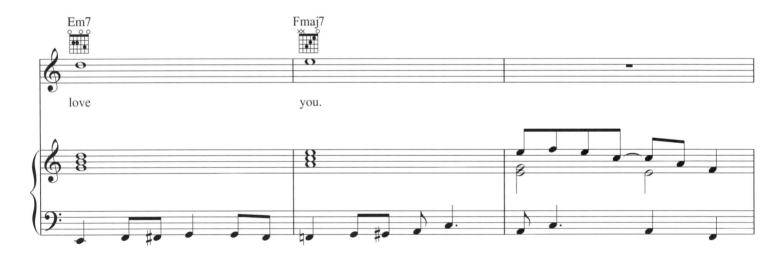

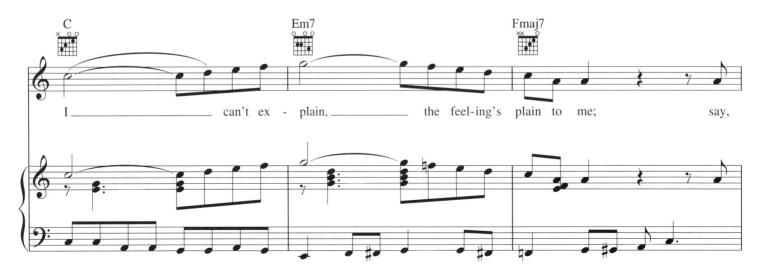

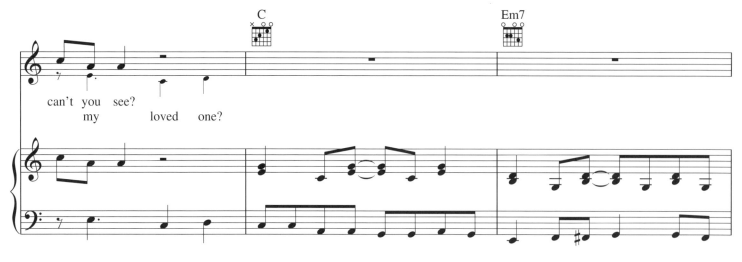

WHEN I GET YOU ALONE

Written by WALTER MURPHY
and ROBIN THICKE

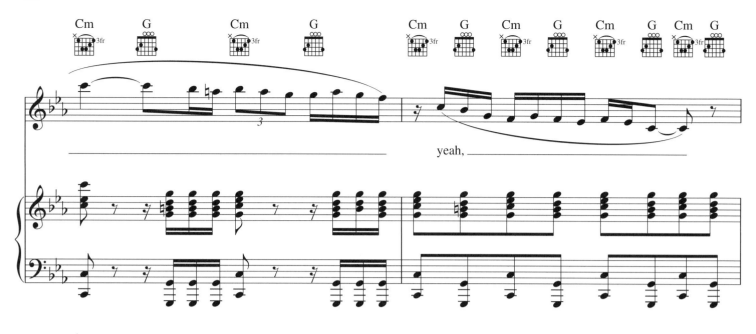

yeah,

yeah.

Additional Lyrics

2. Baby girl, you da shhh...
   That makes you my equivalent.
   Well, you can keep your toys in the drawer tonight,
   All right.
   All my dawgs talkin' fast,
   Ain't you got some photographs?
   'Cause you shook that room like a star, now.
   Yes, you did, oh.

ANIMAL

Words and Music by TIM PAGNOTTA,
TYLER GLENN, BRANDEN CAMPBELL,
ELAINE DOTY and CHRISTOPHER ALLEN

Fast Rock

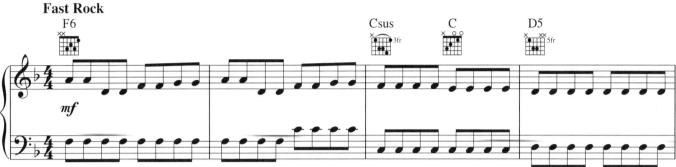

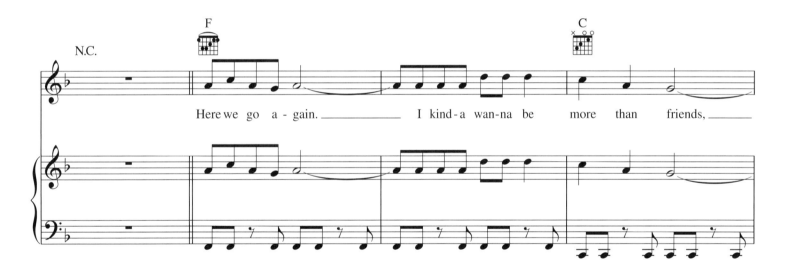

Here we go a-gain. _____ I kind-a wan-na be more than friends, _____

____ so take it eas-y on me. I'm a-fraid you're nev - er sat - is -

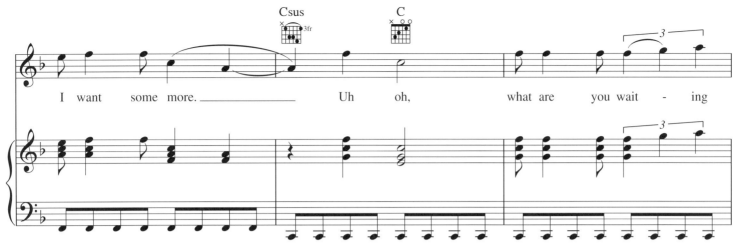

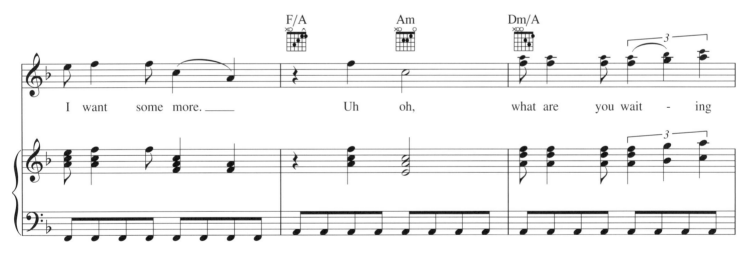

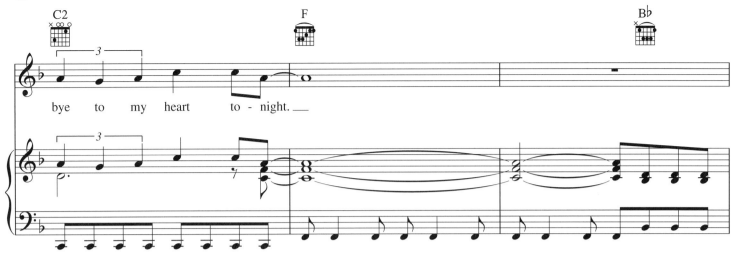

bye to my heart to-night. ___

Here we are a-gain. _____ I feel the chem-i-cals is kick-in' in. ___

___ It's get-ting heav-y and I wan - na run and hide. I

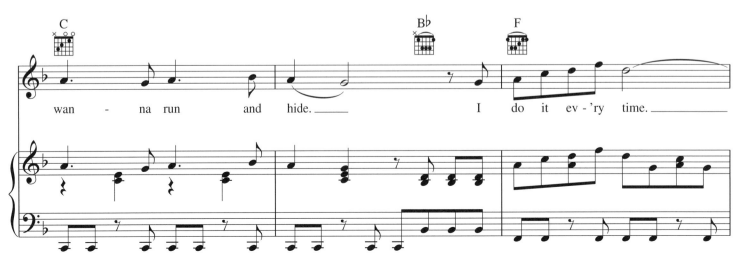

wan - na run and hide. ___ I do it ev-'ry time. ___

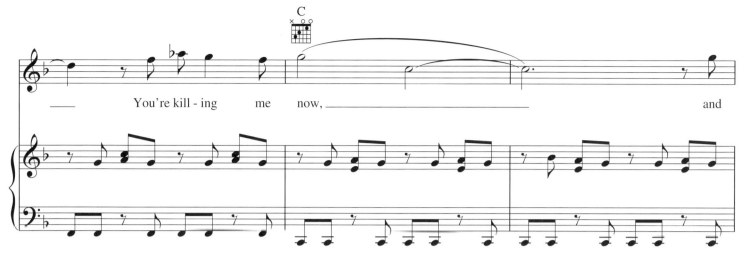

You're kill-ing me now, _____ and

I won't be de-nied __ by you, the an-i-mal in-

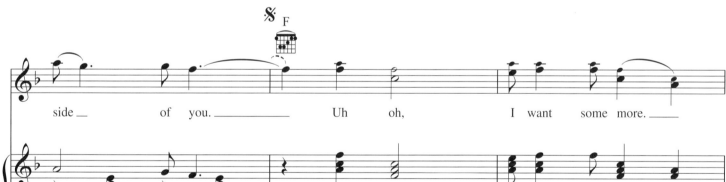

side __ of you. _____ Uh oh, I want some more. _____

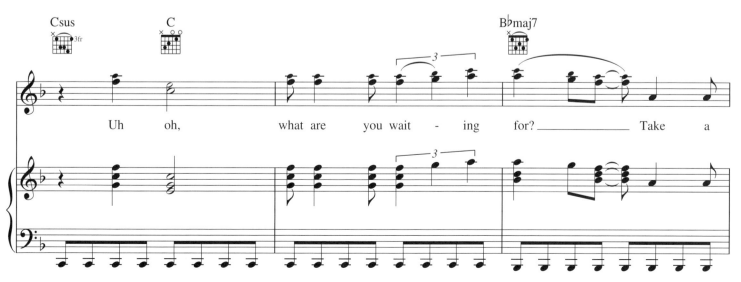

Uh oh, what are you wait-ing for? _____ Take a

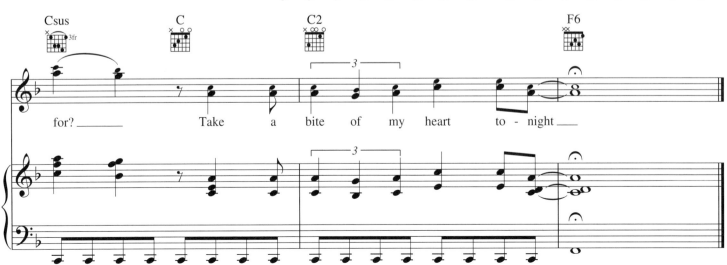

MISERY

Words by ADAM LEVINE
Music by ADAM LEVINE,
JESSE CARMICHAEL and SAM FARRAR

Moderate Funk Rock groove

Oh, yeah. ___ Oh,

yeah. So scared of break-ing it ___ that

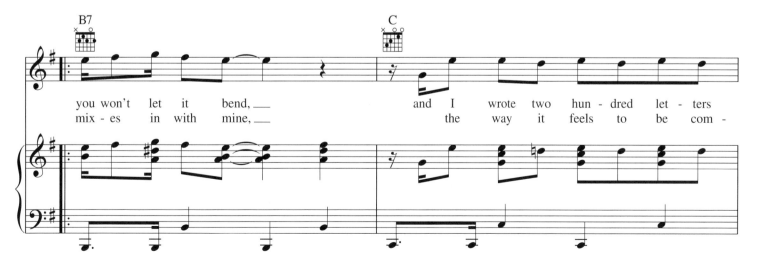

you won't let it bend, ___ and I wrote two hun-dred let-ters
mix-es in with mine, ___ the way it feels to be com-

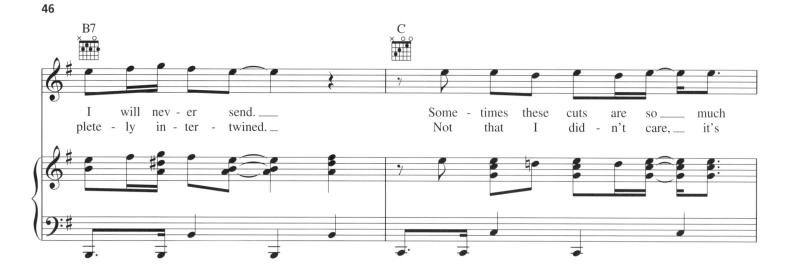

I will nev-er send. ___ Some-times these cuts are so ___ much
plete-ly in-ter-twined. ___ Not that I did-n't care, ___ it's

deep-er than ___ they seem. ___ You'd rath-er cov-er up; ___ I'd
that I did-n't know. ___ It's not what I did-n't feel, ___ it's

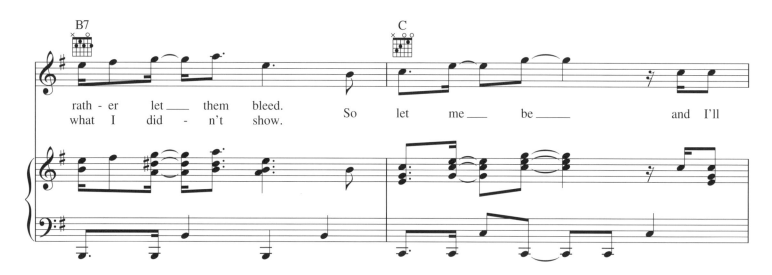

rath-er let ___ them bleed. So let me ___ be ___ and I'll
what I did-n't show.

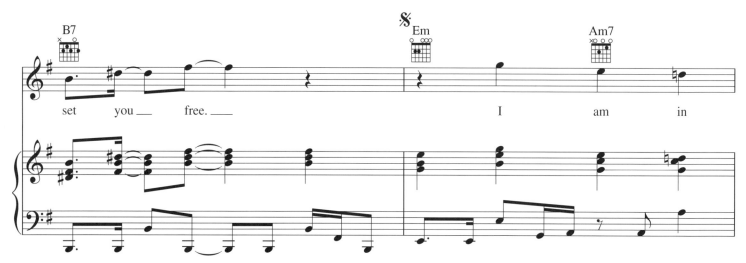

set you ___ free. ___ I am in

mis - er - y. _____ There ain't no - bod - y who can

com - fort ___ me, _____ oh, yeah. ___ Why won't you

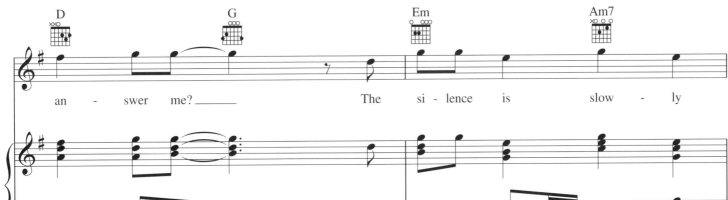

an - swer me? _____ The si - lence is slow - ly

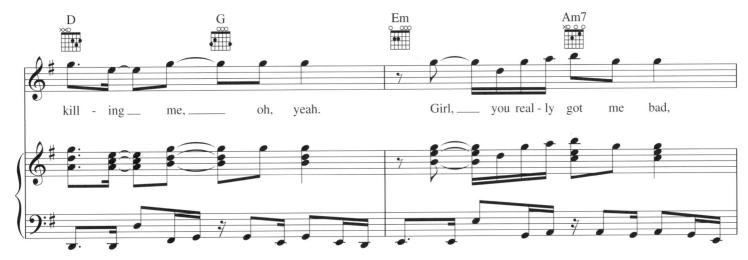

kill - ing ___ me, _____ oh, yeah. Girl, ___ you real - ly got me bad,

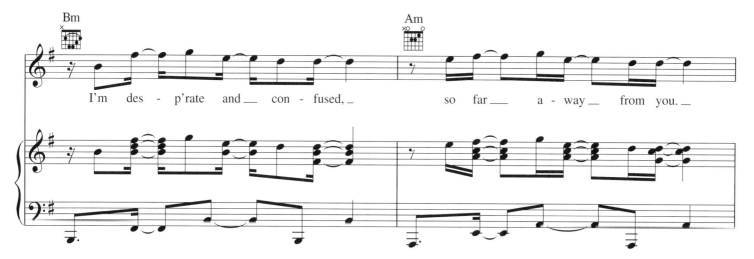

I'm des - p'rate and _ con - fused, _ so far _ a - way _ from you. _

I'm get - ting there. I don't _ care where _ I have _ to run. _

Why do you do what you do to me, yeah?

Why won't you an - swer me, an - swer me, yeah? _ Why do you

do what you do to me, yeah? Why won't you

D.S. al Coda

an - swer me, an - swer me, yeah?

CODA

I'm gon-na get you back, yeah.

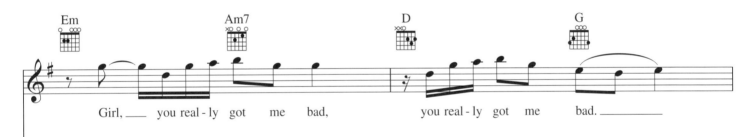

Girl, ___ you real-ly got me bad, you real-ly got me bad. _____

Now I'm gon-na get you back, I'm gon-na get you back.

BLACKBIRD

Words and Music by JOHN LENNON
and PAUL McCARTNEY

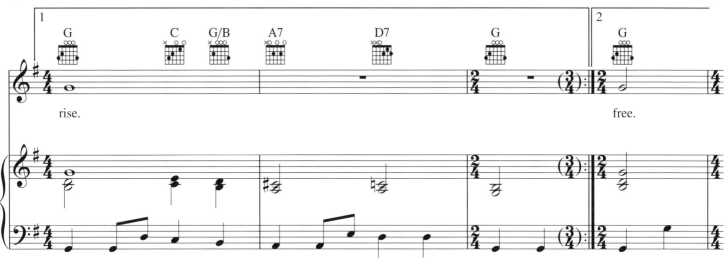

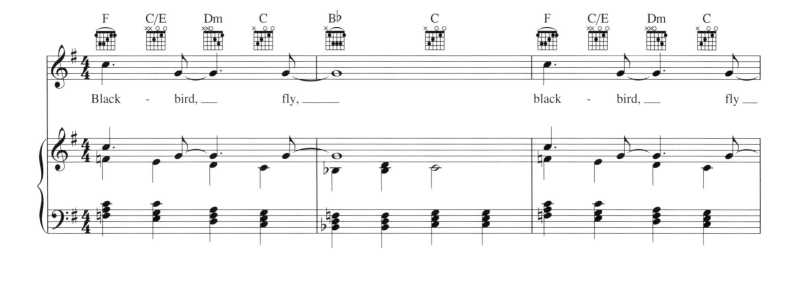

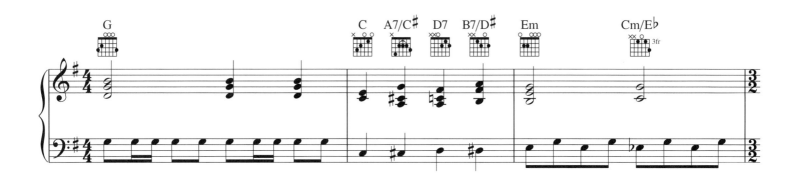

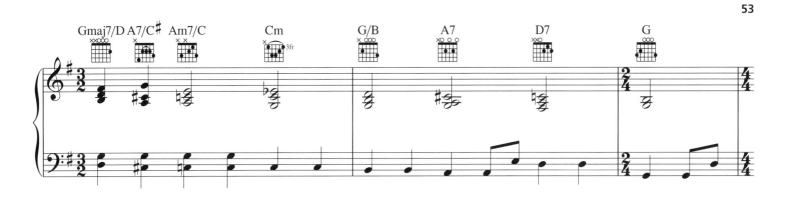

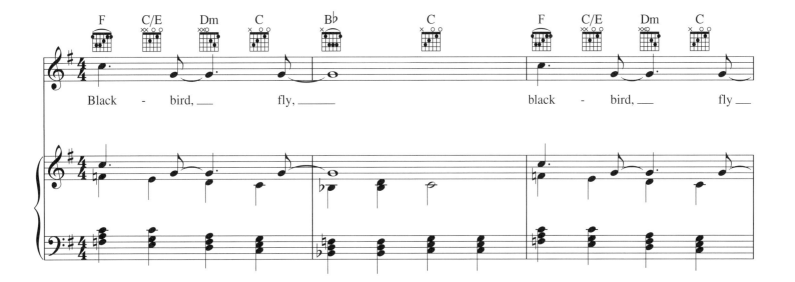

Black - bird, ___ fly, _____ black - bird, ___ fly ___

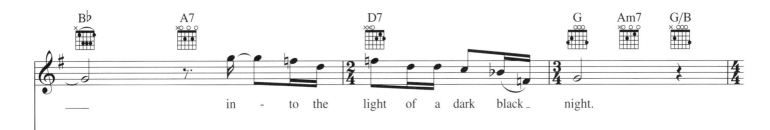

in - to the light of a dark black ___ night.

molto rit. *a tempo*

CANDLES

Words and Music by DAVID KATZ,
CASSADEE POPE, MIKE GENTILE
and SAM HOLLANDER

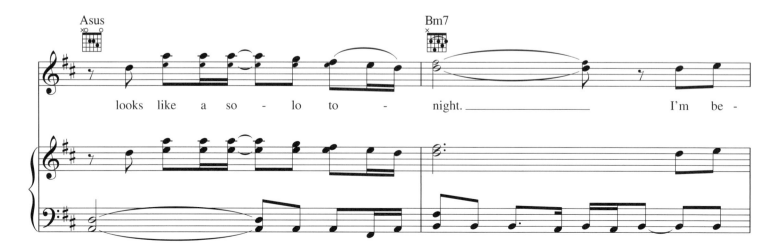

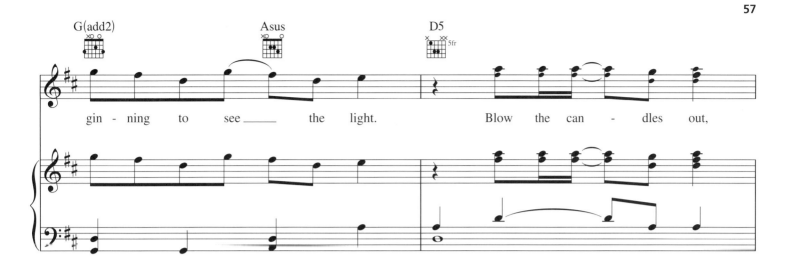

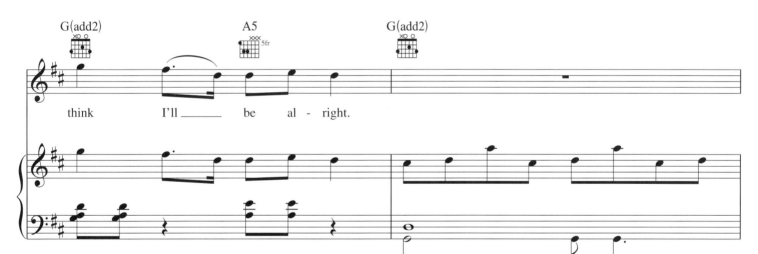

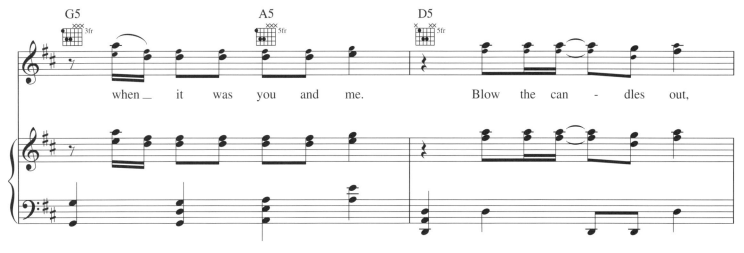

when ___ it was you and me. Blow the can - dles out,

looks like a so - lo to - night. _____ I'm be - gin-ning to see ___ the light.

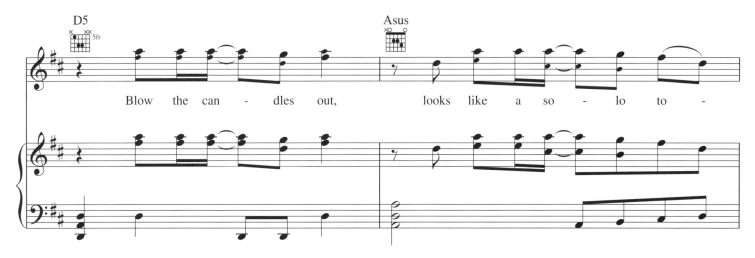

Blow the can - dles out, looks like a so - lo to -

night. _____ But I think I'll _____ be al - right.

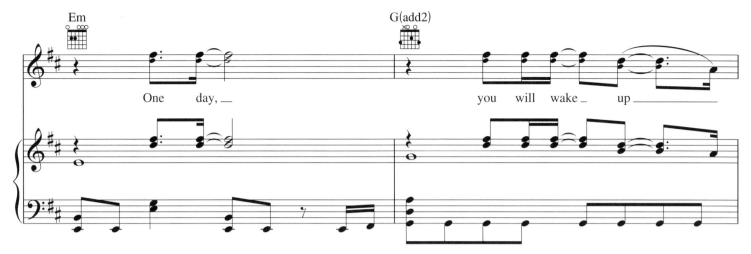

One day, ___ you will wake ___ up _____

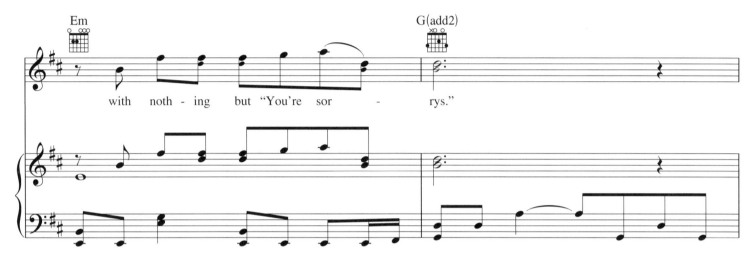

with noth - ing but "You're sor - rys."

And some - day, ___ you will get ___ back

ev - 'ry - thing you ___ gave me. _____

RAISE YOUR GLASS

Words and Music by ALECIA MOORE,
MAX MARTIN and JOHAN SCHUSTER

Where's the ___ rock ___ and ___ roll?
It's so ___ on ___ right now.

Par - ty - crash - er, pen - ny - snatch - er,

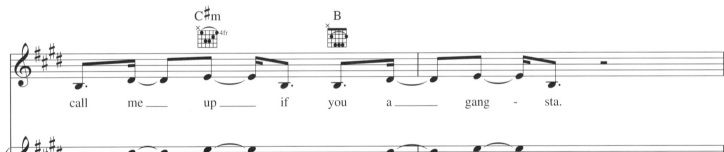

call me ___ up ___ if you a ___ gang - sta.

Don't be ___ fan - cy; just get ___ danc - y.

64

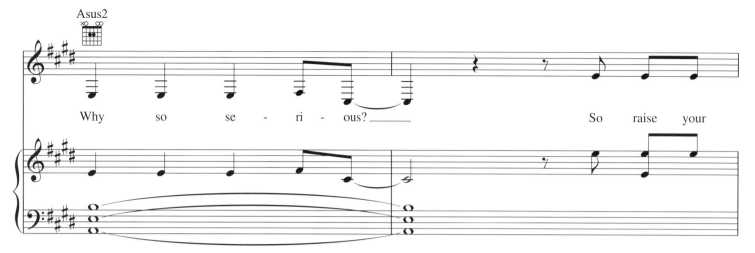

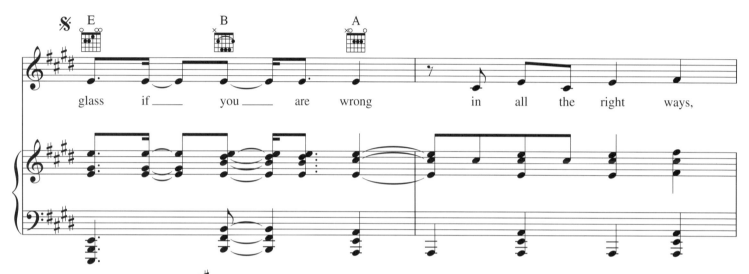

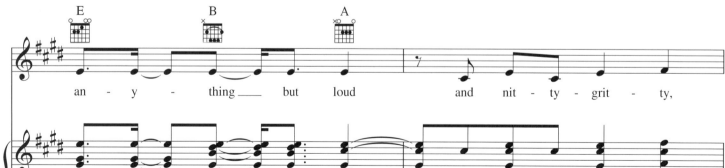

dirt - y ___ lit - tle freaks. Won't you come on and, come on and

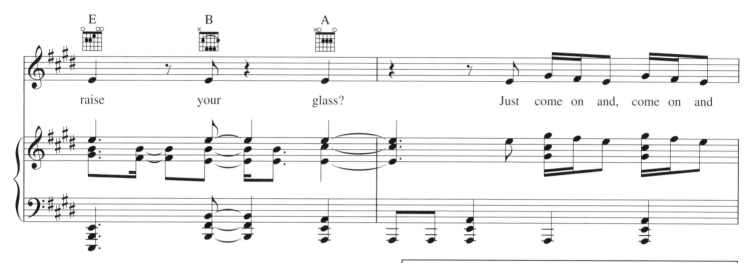

raise your glass? Just come on and, come on and

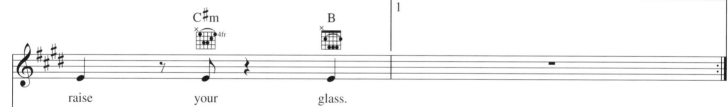

raise your glass.

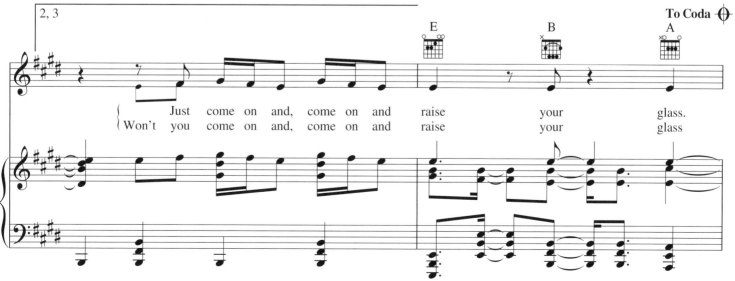

Just come on and, come on and raise your glass.
Won't you come on and, come on and raise your glass

Just come on and, come on and raise your glass.

My glass is empty. *That sucks!*

So if you're too school for cool and you're

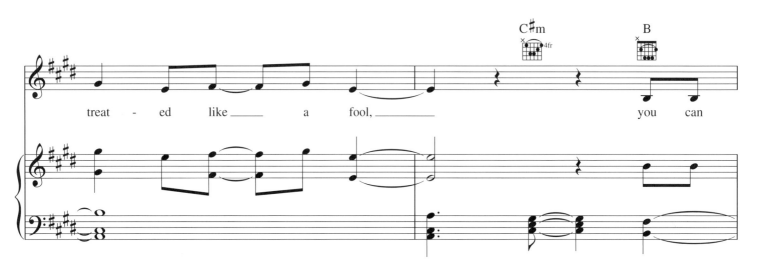

treat - ed like a fool, you can

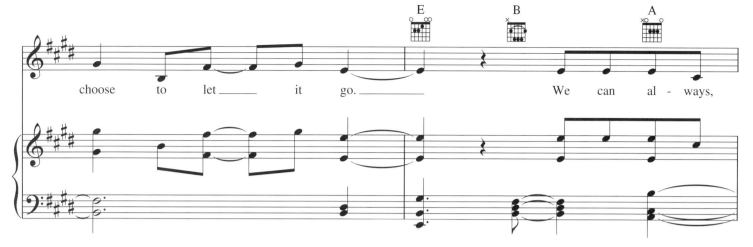

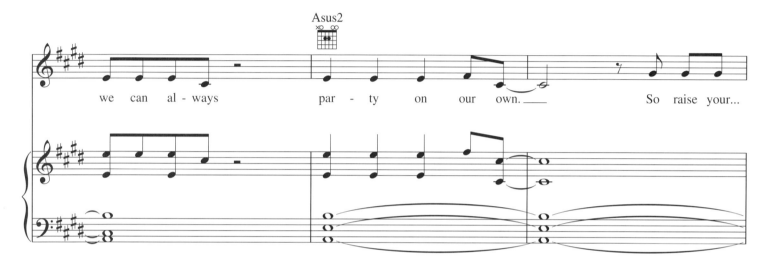

SOMEWHERE ONLY WE KNOW

Words and Music by TIM RICE-OXLEY,
RICHARD HUGHES and TOM CHAPLIN

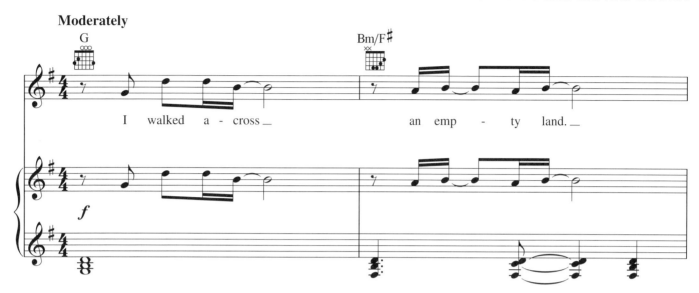

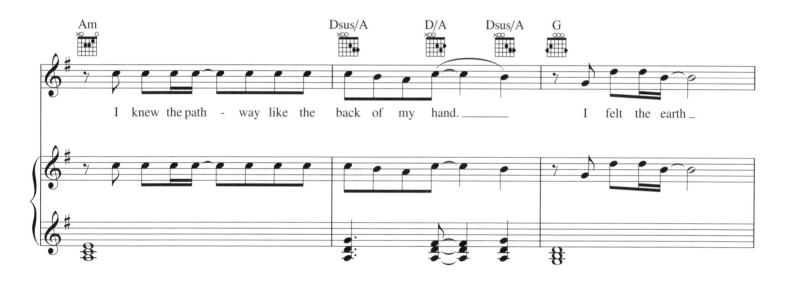

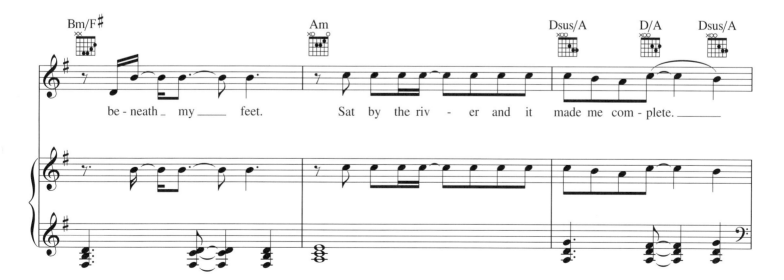

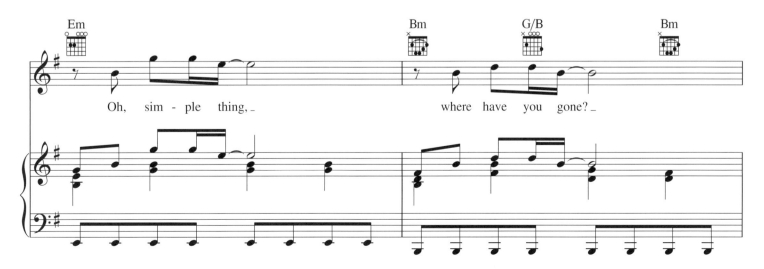

I'm get-ting old and I need some-thing to re-ly on.

So tell me when _ you're gon-na let me in. _

I'm get-ting tired and I need some-where to be - gin. _ And if _ you have a

min - ute, why don't we go _ talk _ a-bout it some-where on - ly we know? _

This __ could be the end of ev - 'ry - thing. _____

So why don't we __ go some-where on - ly we know? _____ Some-

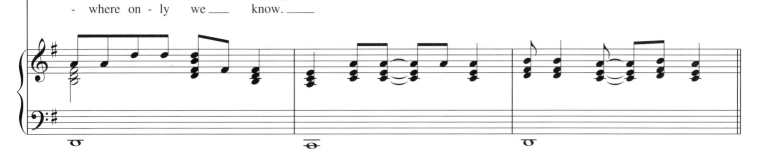

D.S. al Coda

- where on - ly we __ know. ____

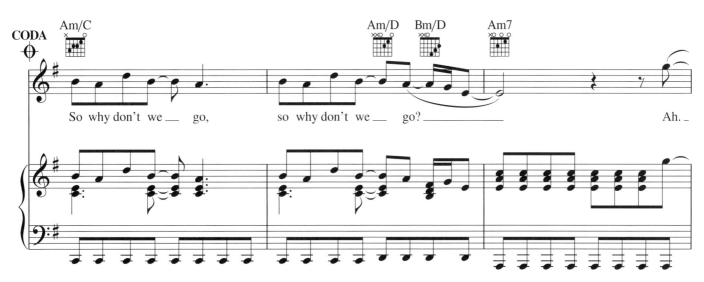

CODA

So why don't we __ go, so why don't we __ go? _____ Ah. __

WHAT KIND OF FOOL

Words and Music by BARRY GIBB
and ALBHY GALUTEN

Moderately slow

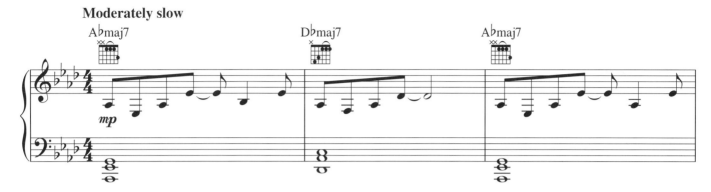

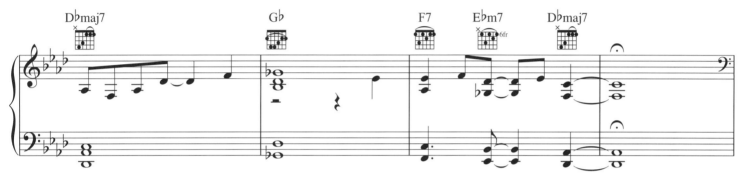

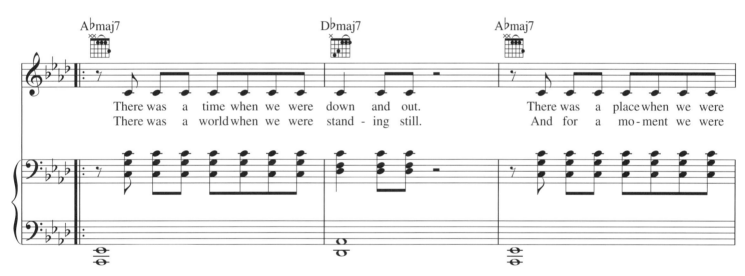

There was a time when we were down and out.
There was a world when we were stand-ing still.

There was a place when we were
And for a mo-ment we were

start-ing o - ver. We let the bough break, we let the heart-ache in.
sep - a - rat - ed. And then you found her, you let the stran - ger in.

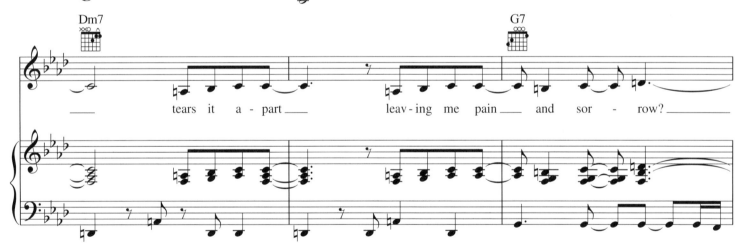

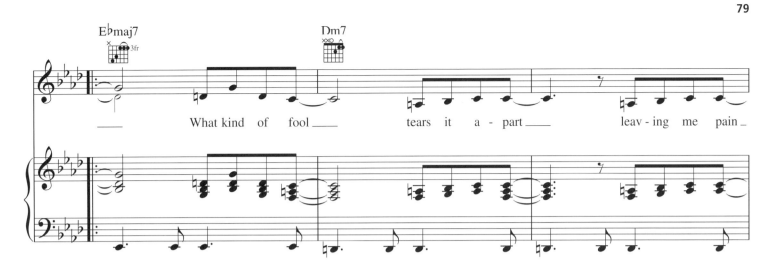

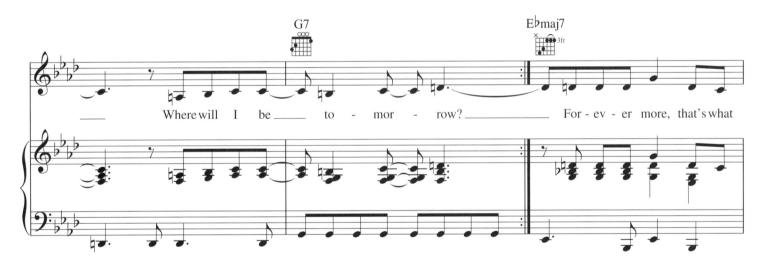

DA YA THINK I'M SEXY

Words and Music by ROD STEWART
and CARMINE APPICE

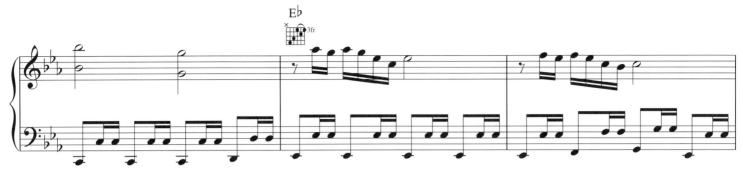

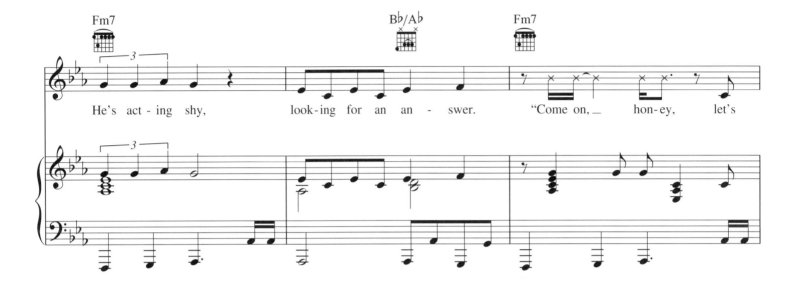

He's act - ing shy, look-ing for an an - swer. "Come on, __ hon-ey, let's

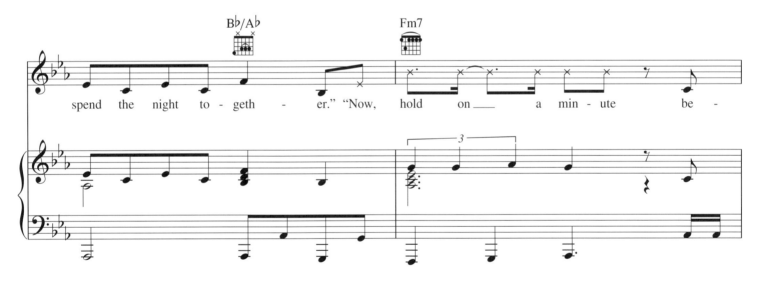

spend the night to-geth - er." "Now, hold on ___ a min-ute be -

fore we go much fur - ther. Give me a dime, so

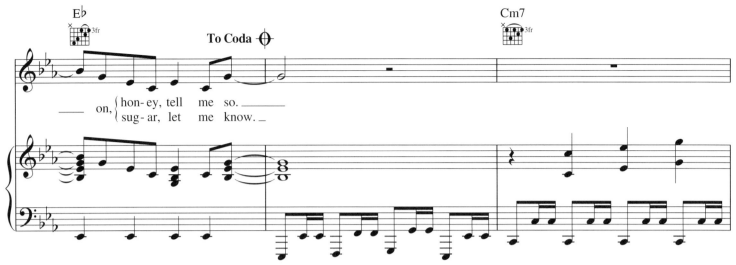

on, { hon-ey, tell me so.
      sug-ar, let me know.

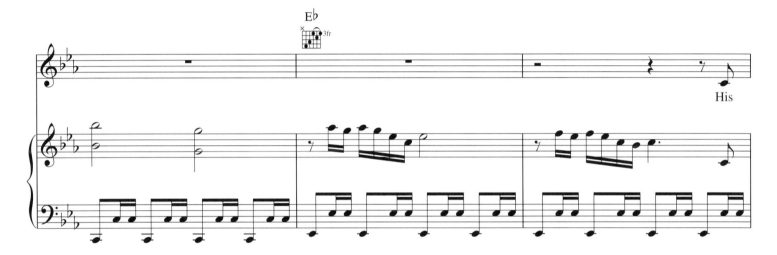

His

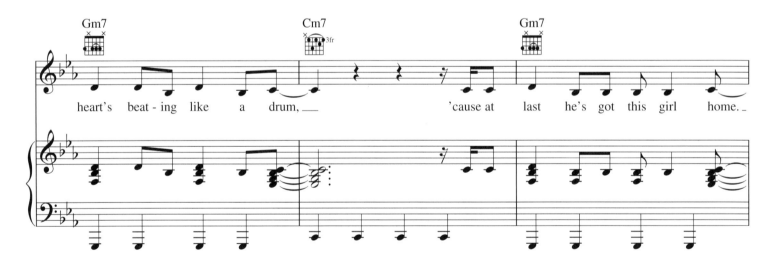

heart's beat-ing like a drum, __ 'cause at last he's got this girl home.

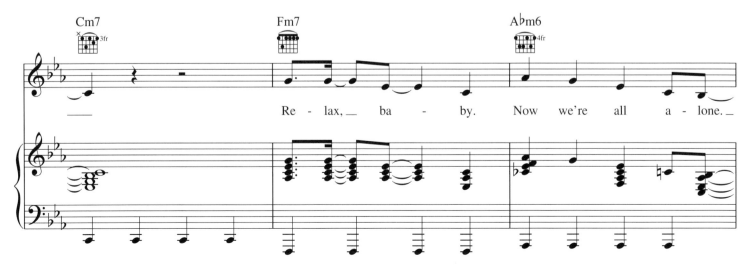

__ Re - lax, __ ba - by. Now we're all a - lone. __

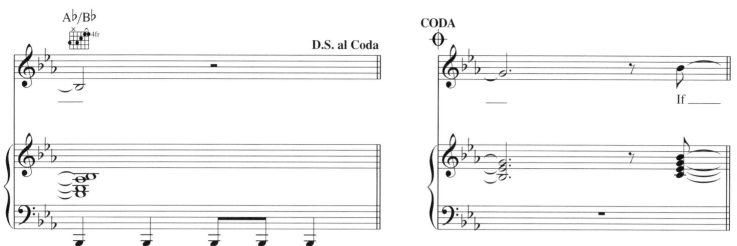

you want my bod - y and you think I'm sex - y, come on, hon - ey, tell me so.

If you real - ly need me, just reach out and touch me. Come

on, sug - ar, let me know. If you want my bod - y.